T0387484

AARON JUDGE

BY REBECCA PETTIFORD

BELLWETHER MEDIA·MINNEAPOLIS, MN

Torque brims with excitement perfect for thrill-seekers of all kinds. Discover daring survival skills, explore uncharted worlds, and marvel at mighty engines and extreme sports. In *Torque* books, anything can happen. Are you ready?

This edition first published in 2024 by Bellwether Media, Inc.

Library of Congress Cataloging-in-Publication Data

Names: Pettiford, Rebecca, author.
Title: Aaron Judge / by Rebecca Pettiford.
Description: Minneapolis, MN : Bellwether Media, 2024. | Series: Sports superstars | Includes bibliographical references and index. | Audience: Ages 7-12 | Audience: Grades 4-6 | Summary: "Engaging images accompany information about Aaron Judge. The combination of high-interest subject matter and light text is intended for students in grades 3 through 7"– Provided by publisher.
Identifiers: LCCN 2023006485 (print) | LCCN 2023006486 (ebook) | ISBN 9798886874600 (library binding) | ISBN 9798886876482 (ebook)
Subjects: LCSH: Judge, Aaron, 1992–Juvenile literature. | New York Yankees (Baseball team)–Juvenile literature. | Baseball players–United States–Juvenile literature.
Classification: LCC GV865.J83 P47 2024 (print) | LCC GV865.J83 (ebook) | DDC 796.357092 [B]–dc23/eng/20230213
LC record available at https://lccn.loc.gov/2023006485
LC ebook record available at https://lccn.loc.gov/2023006486

Editor: Rachael Barnes   Designer: Gabriel Hilger

Printed in the United States of America, North Mankato, MN.

TABLE OF CONTENTS

A NEW RECORD

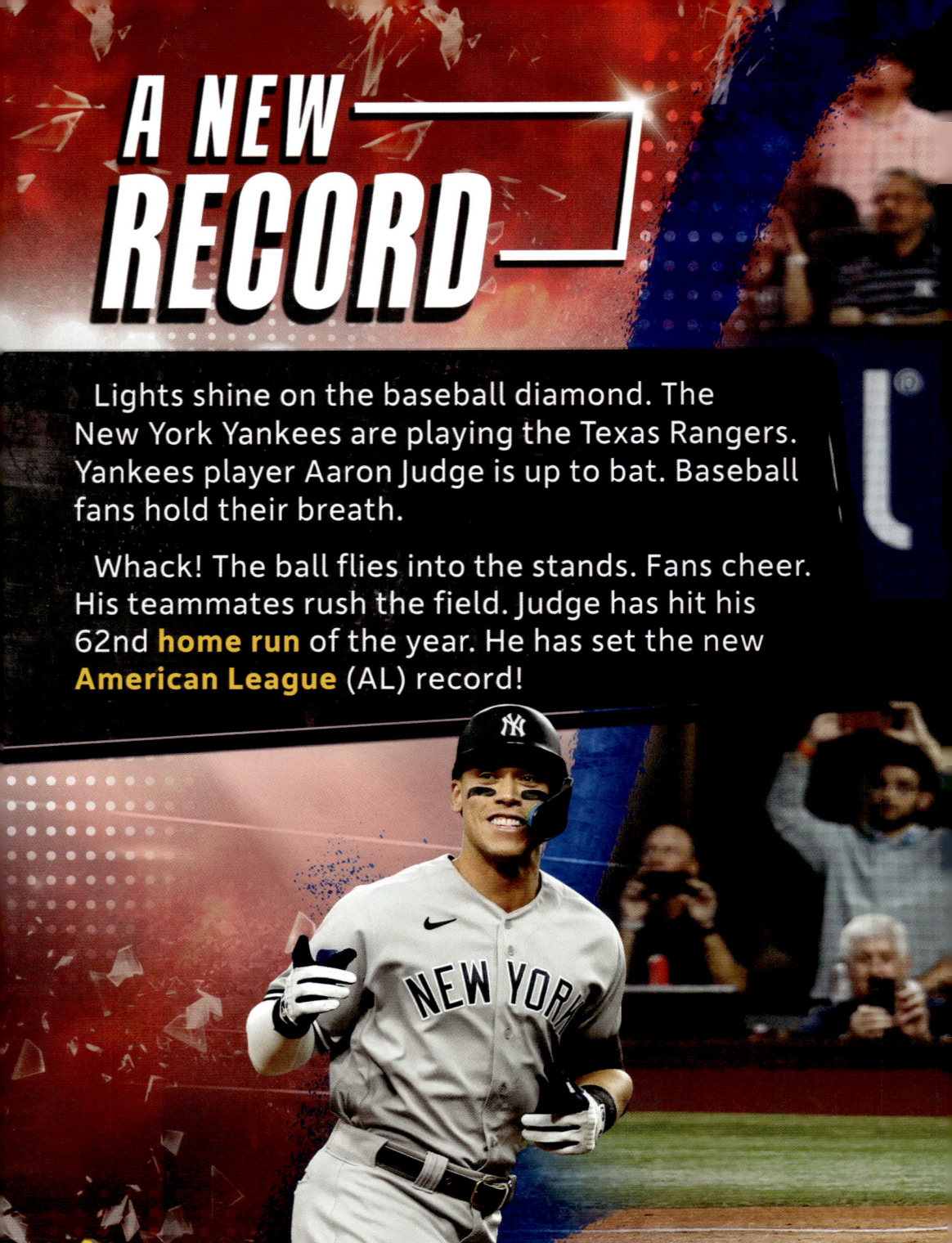

Lights shine on the baseball diamond. The New York Yankees are playing the Texas Rangers. Yankees player Aaron Judge is up to bat. Baseball fans hold their breath.

Whack! The ball flies into the stands. Fans cheer. His teammates rush the field. Judge has hit his 62nd **home run** of the year. He has set the new **American League** (AL) record!

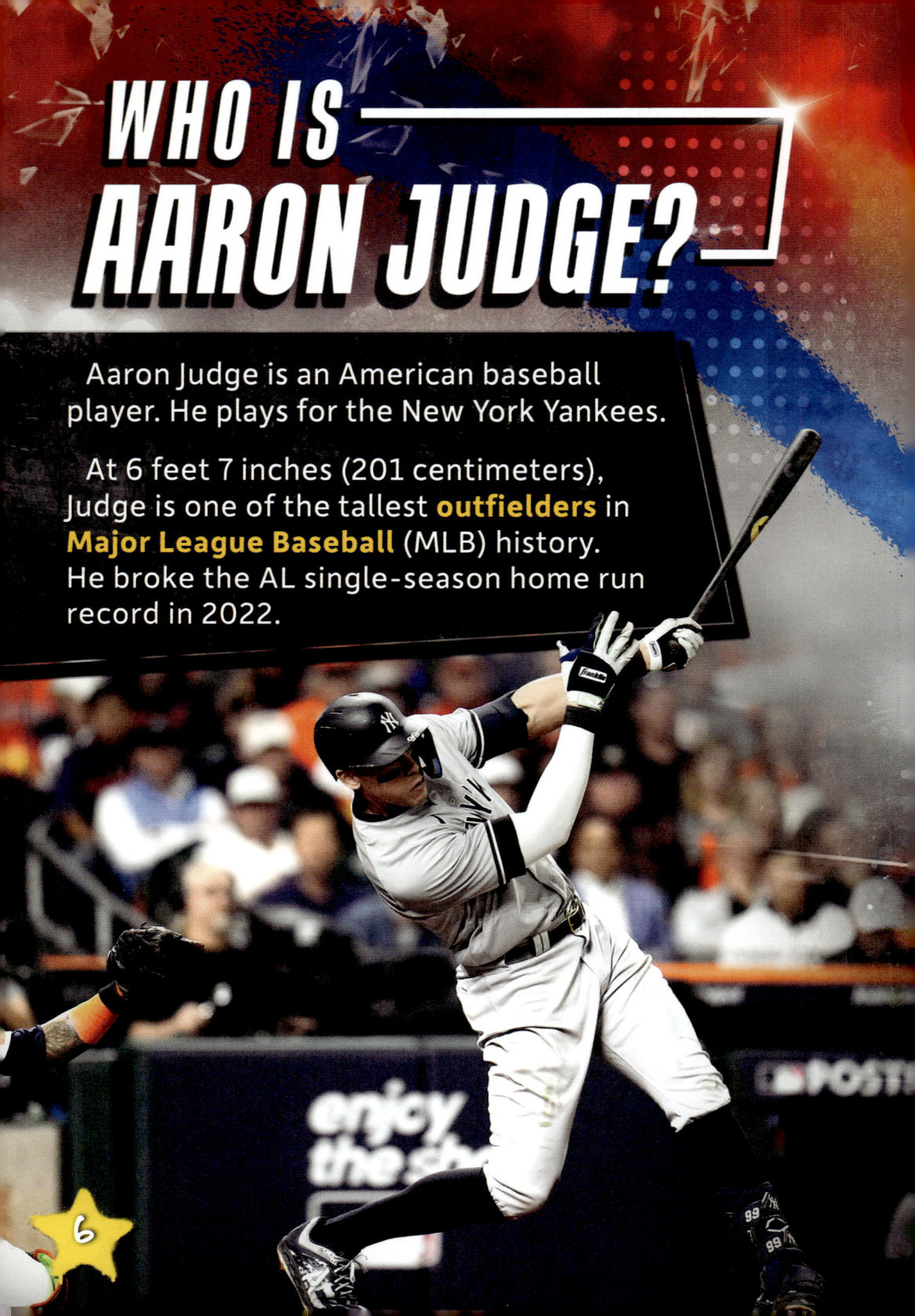

WHO IS AARON JUDGE?

Aaron Judge is an American baseball player. He plays for the New York Yankees.

At 6 feet 7 inches (201 centimeters), Judge is one of the tallest **outfielders** in **Major League Baseball** (MLB) history. He broke the AL single-season home run record in 2022.

AARON JUDGE

BIRTHDAY	April 26, 1992
HOMETOWN	Linden, California
POSITION	outfielder
HEIGHT	6 feet 7 inches
DRAFTED	New York Yankees in the 1st round (32nd overall) of the 2013 MLB Draft

7

THREE-SPORT STAR

Judge was born on April 26, 1992, in Sacramento, California. Wayne and Patty Judge adopted him the day after his birth. His older brother, John, was also adopted.

NUMBER 35

Judge grew up rooting for the San Francisco Giants. His favorite player is Rich Aurilia. As a kid, Judge wore the number 35 to match Aurilia's jersey number.

8

Judge grew up in Linden, California. He was a three-sport star in high school. He played baseball, basketball, and football.

9

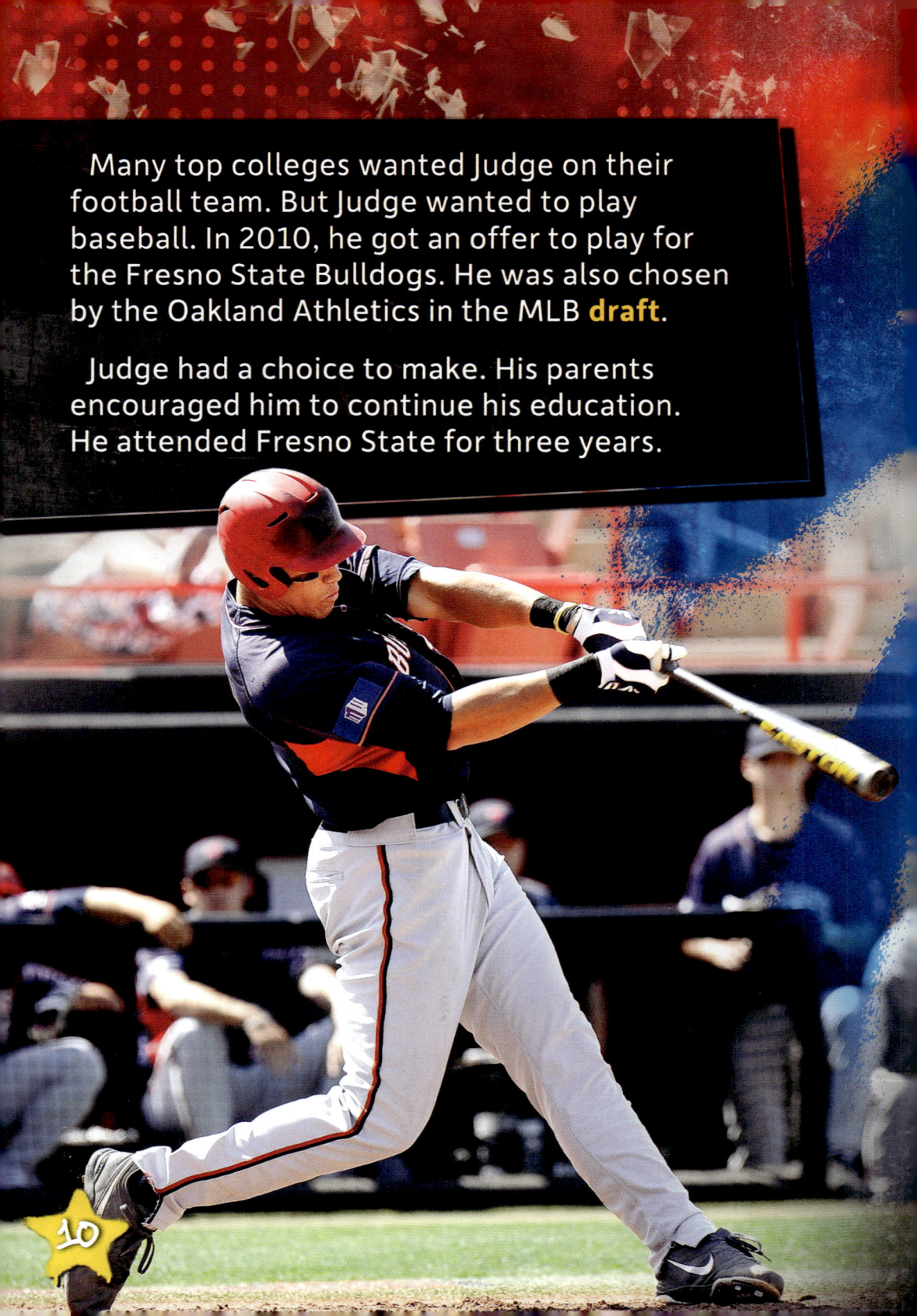

Many top colleges wanted Judge on their football team. But Judge wanted to play baseball. In 2010, he got an offer to play for the Fresno State Bulldogs. He was also chosen by the Oakland Athletics in the MLB **draft**.

Judge had a choice to make. His parents encouraged him to continue his education. He attended Fresno State for three years.

FAVORITES

FOOD

chicken parmesan

ICE CREAM

chocolate chip cookie dough

ANIMAL

penguin

COLOR

purple

11

AWARD-WINNING SLUGGER

2013 MLB DRAFT

In 2013, the New York Yankees selected Judge in the MLB draft. He played for several Yankees **affiliates** from 2014 to 2016. He became known as a powerful batter!

Judge joined MLB on August 13, 2016. He played for the Yankees! But only a month into his MLB career, Judge badly hurt a muscle. He sat out the rest of the season to heal.

12

AARON JUDGE MAP

◎ **Yankee Stadium, The Bronx, New York** **2016** to present

LUCKY GUM

JUDGE POPS TWO PIECES OF BUBBLE GUM INTO HIS MOUTH BEFORE THE FIRST PITCH IN EVERY GAME. HE CHEWS THE SAME TWO PIECES UNTIL HE GETS OUT.

13

2017 HOME RUN DERBY

Judge's first full season as a Yankee was in 2017. He came out swinging! He was named to his first **All-Star Game**. He also won a home run contest called the Home Run Derby.

14

Judge hit 52 home runs in 2017. He was named MLB's **Rookie** of the Year. He also won a **Silver Slugger** award.

NICKNAMES

One of Judge's first nicknames was BAJ. It stands for "Big Aaron Judge." Another popular nickname for him is All Rise.

15

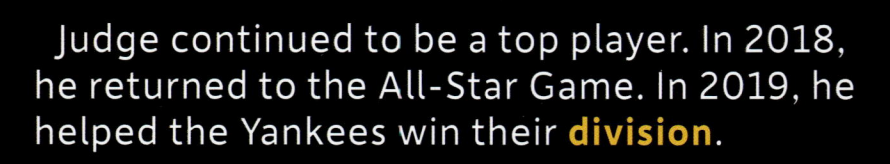

Judge continued to be a top player. In 2018, he returned to the All-Star Game. In 2019, he helped the Yankees win their **division**.

But Judge was often hurt. He missed most of the 2020 season. By 2021, Judge was healed and ready to play. He was chosen to play in the All-Star Game again. He also won his second Silver Slugger.

16

Judge had a record-breaking 2022. With his 62nd home run, he set the AL single-season home run record. He was named the AL **Most Valuable Player** (MVP). He played in another All-Star Game. He also won his third Silver Slugger.

In December 2022, Judge chose to stay with the Yankees. He signed a $360 million, nine-year deal!

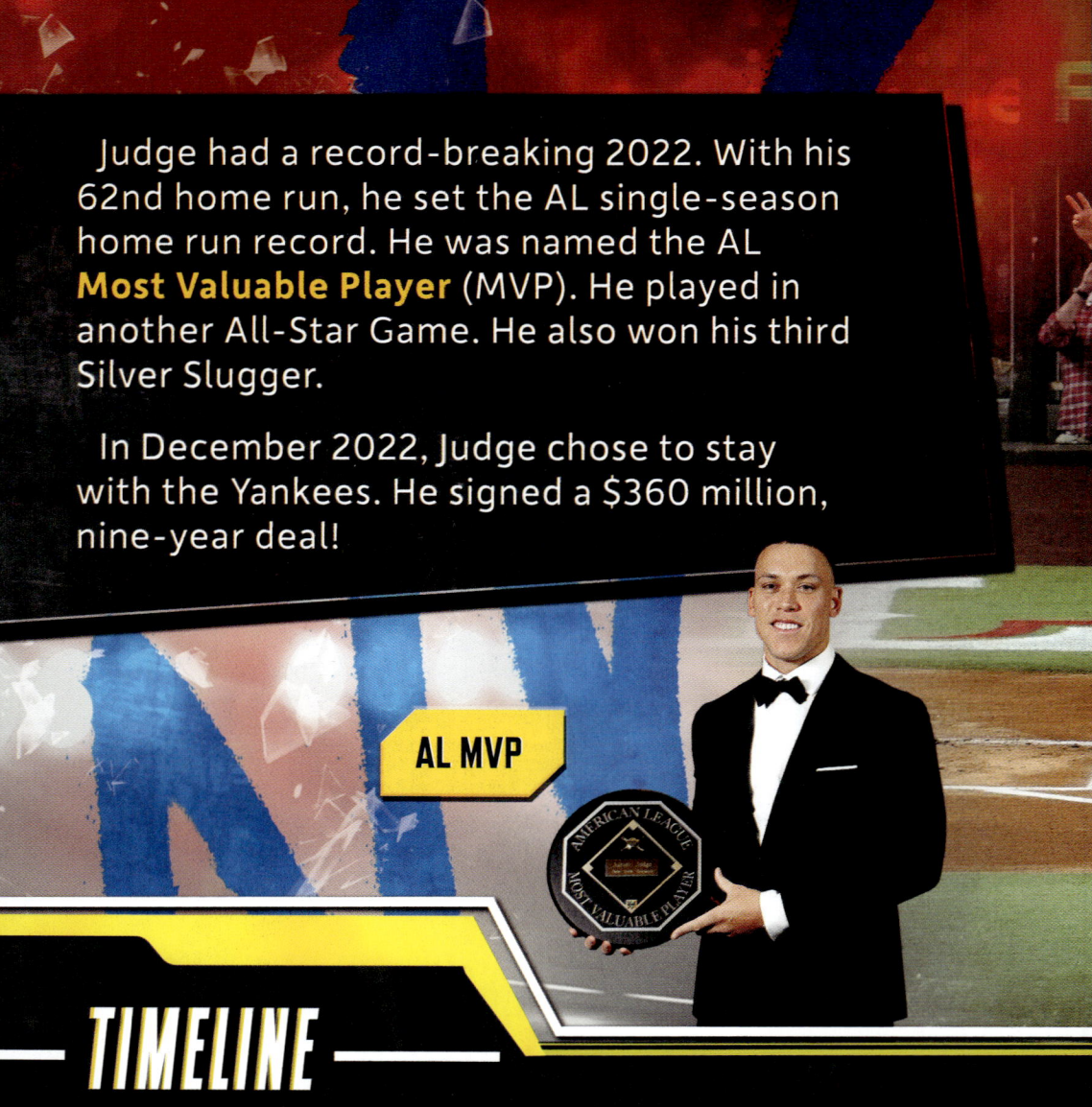

AL MVP

TIMELINE

– 2011 –

Judge joins
the Bulldogs

– 2013 –

Judge is drafted
by the Yankees

18

JUDGE COMPLETING HIS 62ND HOME RUN

— 2016 —

Judge hits his first MLB home run

— 2017 —

Judge wins AL Rookie of the Year

— 2022 —

Judge sets the AL single-season home run record

JUDGE'S FUTURE

In 2018, Judge started the ALL RISE **Foundation**. The organization helps kids to join in activities that help them become responsible people.

20

THE JUDGE'S CHAMBERS

JUDGE HAS HIS OWN SET OF SEATS AT YANKEES' HOME GAMES. IT LOOKS LIKE A COURTROOM. FANS IN "THE JUDGE'S CHAMBERS" SOMETIMES WEAR WIGS!*

As one of the strongest batters in baseball, Judge's future looks bright. Time will tell what awards he will win and what records he will break next!

21

GLOSSARY

affiliates—teams that are owned by another team

All-Star Game—a game between the best players in a league

American League—one of two leagues that make up MLB; the other is the National League.

division—a group of MLB teams from the same area that compete; there are six MLB divisions.

draft—a process during which professional teams choose high school and college players to play for them

foundation—an organization that helps people and communities

home run—a hit where the batter runs all the way around the bases and scores a run

Major League Baseball—a professional baseball league in the United States; Major League Baseball is often called MLB.

most valuable player—the best player in a year, game, or series; the most valuable player is often called the MVP.

outfielders—players that stand far away from the batter to catch baseballs that are hit high into the air

rookie—a first-year player in a sports league

Silver Slugger—an award recognizing the best hitter of each position in baseball

22

TO LEARN MORE

AT THE LIBRARY

Adamson, Thomas K. *Juan Soto*. Minneapolis, Minn.: Bellwether Media, 2023.

Downs, Kieran. *Shohei Ohtani*. Minneapolis, Minn.: Bellwether Media, 2023.

Fishman, Jon, M. *Inside the New York Yankees*. Minneapolis, Minn.: Lerner Publications, 2022.

ON THE WEB

FACTSURFER

Factsurfer.com gives you a safe, fun way to find more information.

1. Go to www.factsurfer.com

2. Enter "Aaron Judge" into the search box and click 🔍.

3. Select your book cover to see a list of related content.

23

INDEX